Countries We Come From

Trinidad and Tobago

by Heather DiLorenzo Williams

Consultant: Marjorie Faulstich Orellana, PhD
Professor of Urban Schooling
University of California, Los Angeles

BEARPORT PUBLISHING

New York, New York

Credits

Cover, © LightFieldStudios/iStock and © Anton_Ivanov/Shutterstock; TOC, © LAURA_VN/Shutterstock; 4, © Homo Cosmicos/Shutterstock; 5T, © John de la Bastide/Shutterstock; 5B, © reptiles4all/Shutterstock; 7, © Claudio306/Shutterstock; 8, © Anton_Ivanov/Shutterstock; 9, © phbcz/iStock; 10, © Wang LiQiang/Shutterstock; 11, © Patrick K. Campbell/Shutterstock; 11T, © Vladimir Wrangel/Shutterstock; 11B, © BasPhoto/Shutterstock; 12, © DebraLee Wiseberg/Getty Images; 13, © Christine Norton Photo/Shutterstock; 14, © Werner Forman Archive Heritage Images/Newscom; 15T, © kavalenkau/Shutterstock; 15B, © Global42/Shutterstock; 16T, © Claudio306/Shutterstock; 16B, © Pcphotography69/Dreamstime; 17, © lidian Neeleman/Shutterstock; 18, © Olesia Bilkei/Shutterstock; 19, © Salim October/Shutterstock; 20, © Marc Guitard/Getty Images; 21, © Randy Brooks/CPL T20/Getty Images; 22, © omgimages/Getty Images; 23, © Lisa F. Young/Dreamstime; 24, © John de la Bastide/Shutterstock; 25, © Blacqbook/Shutterstock; 26T, © picturepartners/Shutterstock; 26B, © jutia/Shutterstock; 27, © Anna_Pustynnikova/Shutterstock; 28, © PeterEtchells/Getty Images; 29T, © Regien Paassen/Shutterstock; 29B, © Lynsey Allan/Shutterstock; 30T, © Andrea De Silva/EFE/Newscom; 30M, © Oleg_Mit/Shutterstock; 30B, © Andrea De Silva/EFE/Newscom; 31 (T to B), © Ivan Smuk/Shutterstock, © lidian Neeleman/Shutterstock, © Claudio306/Shutterstock, © Lynsey Allan/Shutterstock, © kavalenkau/Shutterstock, and © John de la Bastide/Shutterstock; 32, © Boris15/Shutterstock.

Publisher: Kenn Goin
Senior Editor: Joyce Tavolacci
Creative Director: Spencer Brinker
Design: Debrah Kaiser
Photo Researcher: Book Buddy Media

Library of Congress Cataloging-in-Publication Data

Names: Williams, Heather DiLorenzo, author.
Title: Trinidad and Tobago / by Heather DiLorenzo Williams.
Description: New York, New York : Bearport Publishing, [2019] | Series: Countries we come from | Includes bibliographical references and index.
Identifiers: LCCN 2018044352 (print) | LCCN 2018044397 (ebook) | ISBN 9781642802627 (ebook) | ISBN 9781642801934 (library bound)
Subjects: LCSH: Trinidad and Tobago—Juvenile literature.
Classification: LCC F2119 (ebook) | LCC F2119 .W56 2019 (print) | DDC 972.983—dc23
LC record available at https://lccn.loc.gov/2018044352

For more information, write to Bearport Publishing Company, Inc., 45 West 21st Street, Suite 3B, New York, New York 10010. Printed in the United States of America.

10 9 8 7 6 5 4 3 2 1

Contents

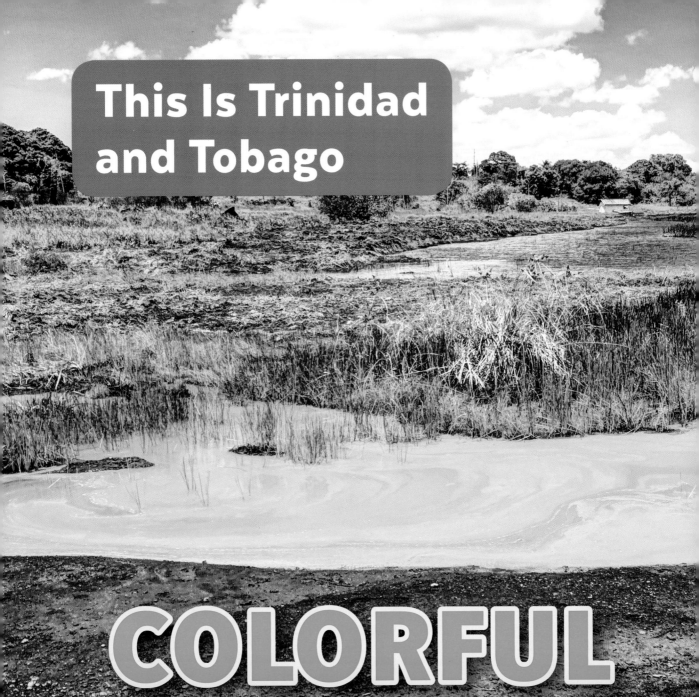

COLORFUL

Creative

Alive

Trinidad and Tobago is a country made up of two main islands.

The islands are located in the Caribbean Sea.

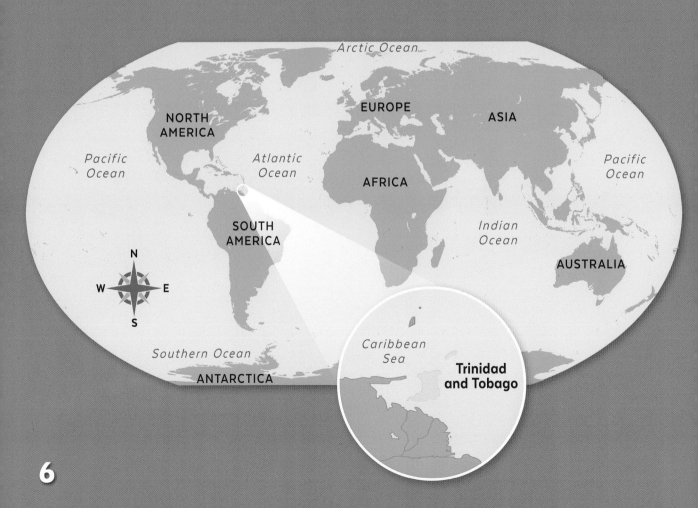

Over one million people live in Trinidad and Tobago.

Trinidad is larger than Tobago.

It has many lakes.

Pitch Lake in Trinidad is made of **asphalt**. It's so thick people can walk on it!

Pitch Lake

Both islands are hilly and have miles of beaches.

9

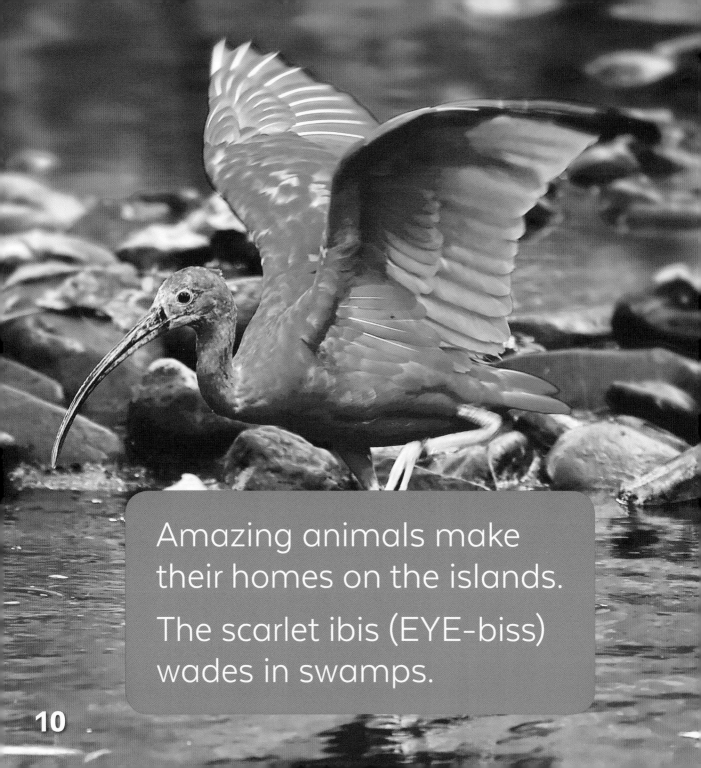

Amazing animals make their homes on the islands.

The scarlet ibis (EYE-biss) wades in swamps.

paca

Pink-toed tarantulas scurry up trees.

Ratlike pacas search for fruit to eat.

The Trinidad motmot bird lives only on Trinidad and Tobago.

11

The **climate** of Trinidad and Tobago is tropical.

There are only two seasons—rainy and dry.

About 67 inches (170 cm) of rain falls in Trinidad each year!

Rainy season is from June to December.
Dry season is from January to May.

13

The Arawaks (AR-uh-wahks) were the first people to live on Trinidad and Tobago.

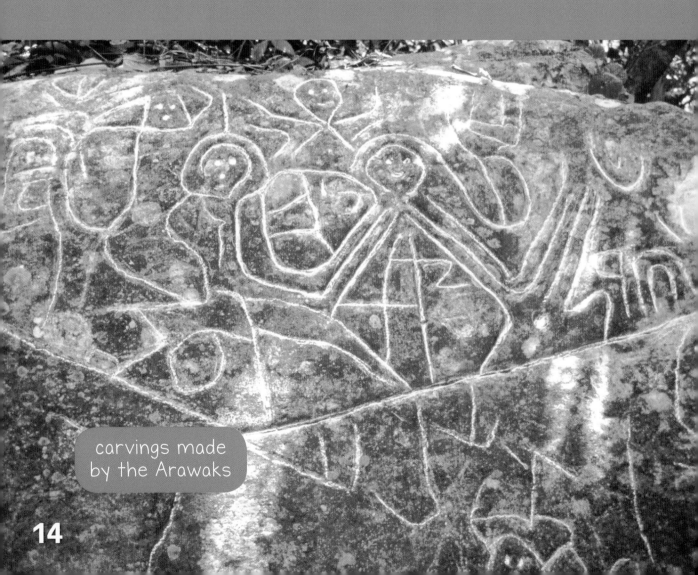

carvings made by the Arawaks

Later, Spain and France fought for control of the islands.

The Spanish **enslaved** many Arawaks.

Great Britain gained power in 1802.

In 1962, Trinidad and Tobago became **independent**.

Christopher Columbus explored Trinidad and Tobago in 1498. He named the islands.

Today, most of the islands' people live in the countryside.

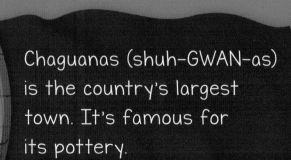

Chaguanas (shuh-GWAN-as) is the country's largest town. It's famous for its pottery.

Other people live in cities. Port of Spain is the country's **capital** city.

English is the main language of Trinidad and Tobago.

People also speak Trinidadian Creole (KREE-ol).

This is how you say *father* in Trinidadian Creole:

Abu (ah-BOO)

This is how you say *mother*:

Ami (ah-MEE)

19

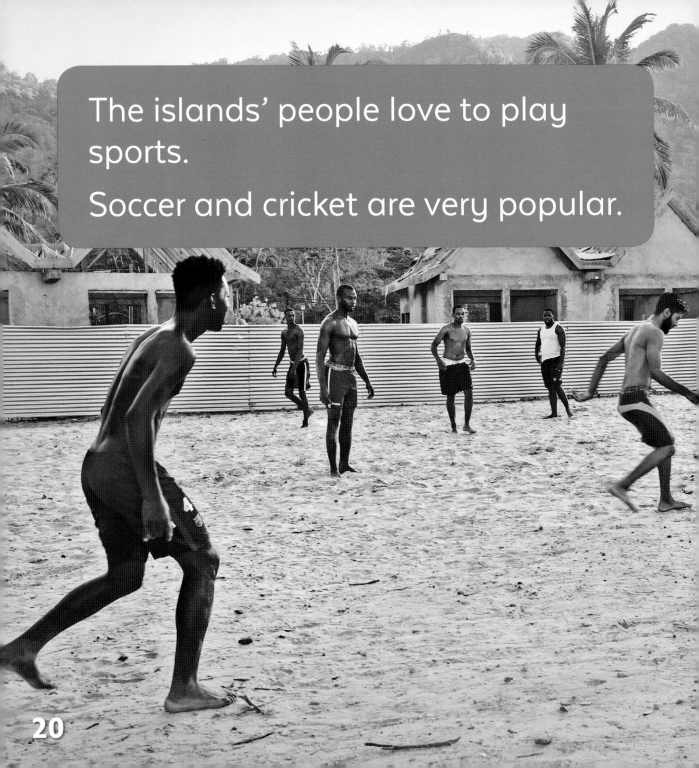

The islands' people love to play sports.

Soccer and cricket are very popular.

Cricket is played with a flat bat and a ball.

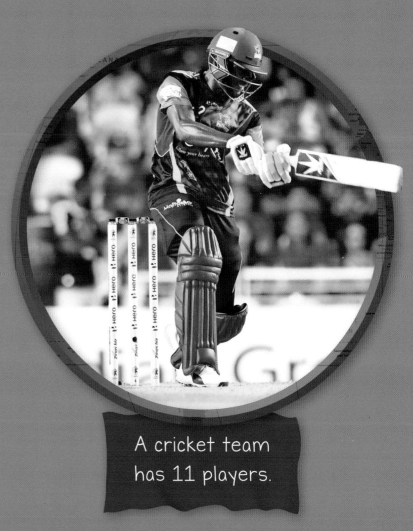

A cricket team has 11 players.

It's time to dance!

The limbo was created by Trinidadians.

People bend backward to pass under a bar.

The person who dips the lowest wins!

steel pan drum

Calypso (kah–LIP–so) is a type of music that started in Trinidad. It's often played with steel pan drums.

Trinidad and Tobago has many festivals.

Carnival (KAR-nuh-val) is the most important one of the year.

People wear colorful costumes.

They sing and dance in the streets.

Moko jumbies are dancers who walk on tall stilts.

stilts

25

This island country is known for its spicy and sweet food.

The scorpion pepper is very hot.

It's so spicy it makes some people cry!

scorpion pepper

jagua fruit

Jagua is a type of fruit that tastes like an apple. Its juice is clear at first but then turns black!

Black cake is a sweet treat.

It's made from almonds, fruit, and burnt sugar.

black cake

Each year, around
400,000 people visit
Trinidad and Tobago.

They enjoy
the beaches
and ocean life.

28

Many go bird-watching.

Will they spot a scarlet ibis?

brain coral

The largest brain **coral** in the world is in Trinidad and Tobago. It's over 16 feet (5 m) wide!

Fast Facts

Capital city: Port of Spain

Population of Trinidad and Tobago:
Over 1 million

Main language:
English

Money: Trinidad and Tobago dollars

Major religion: Christianity

Neighboring countries include:
Barbados, Grenada, and Saint Vincent and the Grenadines

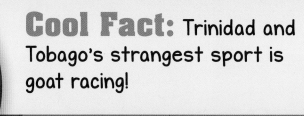

Cool Fact: Trinidad and Tobago's strangest sport is goat racing!

asphalt (AS-fawlt) a thick, black substance used for making roads

capital (KAP-uh-tuhl) the city where a country's government is based

climate (KLYE-mit) the typical weather in a place

coral (KOR-el) a rocklike structure formed by the skeletons of small creatures

enslaved (in-SLAYVD) made someone a servant

independent (in-duh-PEN-duhnt) free of control from others

Index

Read More

Frederick, Malcolm. *Kamal Goes to Trinidad.* London: Frances Lincoln (2010).

Hallworth, Grace. *Down by the River: Afro-Caribbean Rhymes, Games, and Songs for Children.* London: Frances Lincoln (2010).

Learn More Online

To learn more about Trinidad and Tobago, visit
www.bearportpublishing.com/CountriesWeComeFrom

About the Author

Heather DiLorenzo Williams lives in North Carolina. She loves reading and traveling to new places.